Soft Skills and Social Responsibility

The Future of Organizational Leadership

Louis Bevoc

I0505425

Published by
NutriNiche System LLC

Louis Bevoc books...simple explanations of complex subjects

Understanding soft skills

A friend of mine has a daughter named Amy who graduated from a large Midwestern university with a French degree. When Amy was entering the program, her father asked me what I thought about her chosen language major. I said that I thought she would have potential getting a job teaching if she obtained the proper certification, but the thought of her venturing out into the business world did not enter my mind. I believed that business and technology majors were more likely to enter the business world because they had undergone the coursework to do so.

Upon graduation, Amy entered the business world working for a small company researching French documents. Within a year, she accepted a position with a Fortune 500 company where she was the main liaison for all of its French-speaking Canadian plants. After getting experience in a few other areas, she is now in a well-paying and prestigious position as the head of corporate training where she travels the world educating professionals on the French language and culture. After training, these individuals possess the necessary skills to interact with French business people on a professional level. Without this training, hundreds of millions of dollars in business would be jeopardized due to language barriers and lack of cultural understanding.

I was right that Amy would move into teaching, but I was dead wrong about who she would teach and how she would go about it. As the head of corporate training for a Fortune 500 company, her teaching skills and techniques affect thousands of people at all levels of management and expertise. Quite frankly, I did not realize or take into account the soft skills that Amy learned in her French studies at college. These skills helped her adapt to new situations quickly and efficiently while impressing the leaders of her organization as she climbed the corporate ladder. For example, in order to learn a new language during her coursework, Amy had to listen which is a soft skill. She also had to learn proper etiquette and mannerisms, both of which fall under soft skills, when interacting with French people during an internship in Strasbourg, France. She applied these skills in the business world and scaled the corporate ladder into a job that a few decades ago would most likely have been filled by an individual with an MBA (Master's Degree in Business Administration).

Does the above story indicate that a French degree is better than an MBA? Not necessarily, but it does show that change has taken place in leadership thinking about the importance of soft skills. Soft skills are now thought to have a great deal of value in management positions...something that could not have been envisioned in the not so distant past.

The above story is somewhat inspirational for students who prefer to pass on technical or business degrees, but it does not define soft skills. Below is an explanation of soft skills and hard skills for a better understanding of each.

Soft skills

Soft skills are interpersonal in nature and they are used by people to get along with others. Examples include listening, empathy, communication, manners, etiquette, and understanding. These skills can be learned, but they are often innate and are used without a great deal of thought or practice.

Soft skills are not particular to a position, business, or industry. They can be applied to a wide variety of job types and are used by people throughout their professional careers. They are especially useful for leaders because these individuals need to form the relationships necessary to motivate, influence, and guide others. For example, a CEO in the automotive manufacturing business who has empathy and understanding for his employees can have similar empathy and understanding for the employees of a retail chain of health food stores if he assumes the CEO duties in that organization.

Hard Skills

Hard skills are typically learned and can be measured and evaluated. People's proficiency with these skills is usually based on the time and effort they put into learning them. Examples include reading, writing, math, science, accounting, and economics.

Hard skills are often particular to a job, business, or industry. They are very valuable because they help people solve problems that cannot be solved by those who are unqualified. These skills are usually acquired through challenging classroom work and other types of training, but the time and effort put forth are well worth it when the skills are put into action.

One disadvantage of hard skills is the fact that they are often not applicable when leaders make career changes. For example, using the example in the soft skills description above, the strong mechanical engineering skills of the CEO in the automotive manufacturing business will most likely not be helpful in his new role as CEO of the retail chain of health food stores.

A lot more could be discussed concerning hard and soft skills, but the above descriptions give a basic idea of the value of the two concepts. Now, let's move into a more specific discussion about soft skills and their usefulness for leaders.

Leadership and soft skills

The world is made up of all different types of leaders with a variety of different styles. Some leaders are hands-on while others are hands-off, some lead from the front while others lead from behind, and some lead by words while others lead with actions. Specific types of leaders include authoritarian, transactional, transformational, and democratic with each type possessing different traits as shown below.

Authoritarian

These leaders want their organizations to be as efficient as possible, and they believe order and structure are the best way to achieve efficiency. Direct supervision is important and subordinates are kept on a tight leash. Policies and procedures are strictly followed, relationships are professional, and communication always flows from top to bottom.

Authoritarian leaders focus on control. They maintain close supervision so they do not lose control, and they see other types of leadership styles (such as democratic) as inefficient because control is limited.

Transactional

Transactional leaders use rewards and punishment to influence employee behavior. They use rewards when performance meets or exceeds expectations, and they use punishment when performance is below expectations. Rewards are typically monetary, material, or psychological with the idea being simply to recognize performance achievements. Punishment usually involves corrective action and a plan for improvement with the idea being to eliminate the problem and progress toward satisfactory performance.

Transactional leaders believe in rules and standardized practices. They like to develop systems and hold employees accountable for meeting established standards. Unlike other leadership styles, such as democratic, they prefer the status quo and typically do not like change. Efficiency, flow, and productivity rank above everything else, and the best way to maximize these variables is to establish goals and objectives.

Transformational

Transformational leaders are typically knowledgeable and charismatic. They work tirelessly to get personnel to think independently about what is best for the organization. This is accomplished by setting objectives that drive employees to work harder and increase performance. In short, the goal of this leadership style is to "transform" employee thinking so they want to work toward improving the organization and taking it to the next level.

Democratic

Democratic leaders share decision making responsibilities with other employees. They believe in debate and encourage discussion. This leadership style allows employees to feel good about themselves and the fact that they are involved in decision-making processes. Democratic leaders view authoritarian leadership as too rigid with no room for new ideas or creativity.

The skills of the above leaders can be soft or hard, and this book will show why people with soft skills often make the most successful leaders. Below are some important traits of soft skilled leaders that show why they are good at motivating others to follow them.

True listeners

Much of what humans learn is acquired through listening. Reading, writing, and speaking account for some learning, but listening is the biggest factor.

Unfortunately, people comprehend less than half of what they hear. This means the majority of time spent listening is wasted...at least from a learning standpoint. Based on this, it seems rather obvious that people would try to improve their listening skills. However, this is typically not the case, and that is why effective listeners often rise to leadership roles in organizations.

Some of the benefits of listening include those shown be ow.

Understanding

There is no doubt that effective listening creates a better understanding of the discussion that is transpiring. Without understanding, most conversations are severely hindered. Think about holding a conversation with a friend inside a crowded bar that has loud music playing. The loud music and crowd noise creates a barrier to effective listening, and the resulting lack of understanding hinders the conversation.

Efficiency

When people listen to each other, everything becomes more efficient. They understand what is being said, and that understanding results in less confusion and mistakes. In this sense, it is much easier to accomplish goals and tasks that are a part of everyday life.

Insight

When people hear what is actually being said, they gather information that can be used to define their position and make decisions. This information influences behavior and brings about change that helps individuals reach the mindset where they feel the most comfortable. People who do not effectively listen fail to acquire information, and they are often left uncertain of the direction they need to take on important aspects of the conversation. In short, people who listen effectively gain insight that benefits them.

Bonding

This is likely the least known benefit of effective listening, but it is often the most important because trust builds when one person believes another is listening to them...and trust leads to bonding.

Conversations also become more enjoyable when effective listening is employed because there is less repeating of what has already been said. In this regard, effective listing helps people bond because speakers feel like their words are important and not easily forgotten. They do not get annoyed from being asked to repeat the words that they have just spoken, and this prevents the potential conflict that can occur when people become upset with others for apparent lack of interest or concern.

Soft skilled leaders do an excellent job of listening. They stand out among good listeners because they are truly focused on what others are saying with the hope of learning something new. In other words, they are more than just empathetic and understanding...they are also interested.

Soft skilled leaders also know that there is a difference between hearing what someone says and actually listening to what they say. They know how to listen and use that ability to get people to truly feel as if they are being heard.

Conflict resolvers

It can be said with confidence people who lead are going to experience conflict among those who follow them. A harmonious and disagreement-free workplace would be nice, but it is not reality regardless of the type or size of the organization being led.

Contrary to what some people believe, conflict is not all bad. In fact, some conflict is good because change evolves from it. Without disagreement, the status quo would remain the same and nothing would improve. However, conflict can get out of control and become dysfunctional. Dysfunctional conflict is destructive because position becomes more important than principle, and people are attacked instead of problems. These personal attacks are always negative, and nothing constructive gets accomplished.

When dysfunctional conflict occurs, it needs to be resolved. Soft skilled leaders realize the importance of focusing on the problem rather than the people in the conflict, and they work toward a resolution using mitigation strategies that soften the harsh effects and save face for all parties involved. Sometimes these strategies involve negotiation, which is another important trait of soft-skilled leaders as s shown in the next section.

Negotiators

Negotiation is a process where differences among people are settled with some type of agreement. It is necessary when people have dissimilar viewpoints on a given situation, and it usually requires compromise from both sides of the table before an agreement is reached. People are not always happy with the results of a negotiation process, but those results do provide direction for the way things will proceed in the future.

Negotiation is an important trait for any leader because it works well as a tool for goal accomplishment. The "give and take" mentality of the negotiation process allows for each party to give up something for something else that they see as being more important. In business, negotiation often makes or breaks deals and it has the potential to make people rich or destroy them financially.

The best negotiators are those who create win/win situations where each party in the negotiation feels like they have accomplished something of value. This sense of accomplishment allows everyone to leave the negotiation table on good terms, prevents the feeling of being cheated or scammed, and opens the door to future negotiations.

Unfortunately, some people do not believe in compromise. They think they are right, the opposite side is wrong, and the only option is a win for them and a loss for their opponent. Win/lose situations are typically not good because they establish clear cut winners and losers. They do not allow losers to "save face" which can create communication barriers that are difficult, if not impossible, to remove. Losers might be too mad or embarrassed to face winners, so the two parties never again work together on anything.

Since communication and understanding are innate to soft-skilled leaders, it is not surprising that they are able to create win-win situations and distinguish themselves as excellent negotiators. They know how to work with people so both sides of the table get something that they need while giving up something that the other side desires.

Mind openers

Mind opening leaders are individuals who are able to open up the minds of their employees so they will accept things that are outside of their comfort zones. This is a skill that most people do not have and it is very valuable for getting people to embrace change.

Change is difficult for most people to embrace because it requires them to think or behave differently than they have in the past. They have to leave familiar territory and enter into something unfamiliar while not really knowing what lies ahead. For example, Maria changes careers and enters a new field where she must leave behind what she knows and take on new roles and responsibilities. She realizes that her work world is going to change, but she does not know how drastic that change will be. Questions flow through her mind causing her to worry about the future. Examples of these questions include the following:

- Will she understand her new job so she can perform as expected?
- Will she have the respect of coworkers who know that she has no direct experience?
- Will she be able to adjust to a different work environment?
- Will she be able to transfer her skills to her new career?

All of the above questions stem from a fear of the unknown. Overcoming that fear is a daunting task for Maria, but a soft skilled leader can make the process much more fluid and comfortable for her by listening to her, showing empathy for her concerns, and offering support for getting her through the initial phases. Once she settles into the position and has a better understanding of her work environment and job responsibilities, her fears will ease and she will become a productive member of the organization.

Mind opening is one of the most important traits of soft skilled leaders due to the resistance that so many people have to change. They will go to great lengths to avoid leaving the areas of comfort that they have established over time, and they require help outside of themselves to move in a different direction...even if that direction leads to making their jobs easier in the future.

Acceptors

Good leaders act as mind openers for others, but they also need to be open-minded themselves. This means they have to accept the reality of their surroundings. In fact, it is difficult for people to become effective leaders in organizations if they do not accept the reality of situations around them. Adolph Hitler, for example, forced his military personnel to fight till the death even though they had limited equipment and supplies and World War II was at a point where Germany had no chance of emerging victorious. He refused to see his country's defeat as it unfolded around him, regardless of what he personally witnessed or was told by his top aides. In the end, he failed miserably in his leadership role and millions of people were killed or had their lives negatively disrupted.

Hitler, however, was not known as a soft skilled leader. Empathy and understanding are two traits that do not come to mind when thinking about him and, as shown in the preceding paragraph, he was not a particularly good listener. However, there are many other leaders who do have soft skills, and those skills allow them to accept the reality that occurs around them. They hear what other people are telling them, show respect for their opinions and comments, and act accordingly based on an analysis of the entire situation. They experience success in leadership roles because they have the ability to:

Accept problems

Like other leaders, soft skilled leaders understand that problems are going to arise that need to be resolved. However, their skill sets set them apart from other leaders because they have the ability to take things in stride and move toward a resolution without exaggerating the impact of the problem or placing blame on others. On the surface, this ability might not appear to be of any great importance. However, appearances can be deceiving as is the case here because problem exaggeration and blame games in organizations result in compounded issues including unnecessary stress, mental fatigue, fear of job loss, and, if allowed to fester, an exodus of good employees.

The acceptance of problems also helps speed up the time required to find a solution because less time is spent arguing over who is at fault. In business, time is money...and money is what typically drives the bottom line.

Accept criticism

The acceptance of criticism does not come easy for many people. In fact, some individuals are simply not able to handle any type of critique of their actions regardless of the fact that the critique might be constructive. These people cannot get past the feeling of being personally attacked so they refuse to accept suggestions for improvement and, consequently, fail to get better.

Soft skilled leaders allow themselves to be criticized by others without becoming emotionally charged or seeking vengeance against their accusers. They avoid reacting in a hostile or aggressive manner to criticism, and they do not assume that those doing the criticizing are automatically wrong.

The acceptance of criticism helps leaders in two different ways. First, it allows them to improve their leadership skills by understanding their shortcomings and using that understanding to strengthen their weak areas. Second, it improves their image in the minds of others because they are not viewed as being know-it-alls who can do no wrong.

Accept opinion

Everyone has an opinion and rarely, if ever, are those opinions the exact same for a topic of discussion. Keeping this in mind, people should understand that others are not always going to agree with their thinking so they should show respect for differing opinions.

Unfortunately, this is not always the case...especially when the discussion includes race, religion, or politics. However, regardless of the discussion topic, some people always believe their opinion is right and they refuse to spend any time entertaining the possibility that others might be correct.

Soft skilled leaders respect the opinions of others. They do this by understanding that opinions are nothing more than personal thoughts. They also move away from trying to rationalize other's opinions in their own minds because they know that this might not be possible to do.

The acceptance of other's opinions is important for leaders because they open themselves up to new concepts and ideas that they might not think of on their own. It also prevents them from being surrounded by people who never want to disagree or express their own thoughts and ideas.

Soft skilled leaders keep their minds open at all times. They pay attention to their surroundings and know that others possess a world of information that is of no value to them if they choose to ignore it. Quite simply, they view their minds as parachute because those minds "do not work unless they are open."

Change implementers

Change is inevitable for organizations or they will become stagnant and, over time, cease to exist. Change is important for organizational prosperity, and astute leaders understand this importance better than anyone else. They have the ability to visualize what needs to be done for the growth of their organizations. That visualization, however, requires implementation before the change becomes a reality...and only the best leaders successfully complete that implementation.

Change implementation requires mind opening skills in order to get people to buy into the idea of doing something differently, but it also requires the ability to move the process forward and help it take root until it becomes a normal part of the status quo. Soft skilled leaders have this ability due to their influential personalities and communicative styles. They are able to take employees down new trails that lead to unfamiliar territories because they understanding people. Their empathetic nature provides support for those who are unsure of their own actions or the actions of others as the change takes place. The comfort level experienced by employees allows them to become an active part of the implementation process which greatly aids leaders in reaching organizational goals and objectives.

In a nutshell, soft skilled leaders are able to identify where and when change is needed, but, even more importantly, they are able to implement that change so it becomes part of their employees' everyday routines. The key to this implementation is effective communication, something that comes naturally to leaders with soft skills.

Motivators

The phrase "location, location, location" is frequently used to describe real estate transactions because the value of a property is largely based on the area where that property is located. The same idea relates to leaders when trying to get people to follow them, but the phrase is different. Leadership is based on "motivation, motivation, motivation" because people need to be motivated in order to do what those at the top want them to do.

Employees need motivation for a variety of different reasons. One person needs it for undergoing change while another needs it for confidence-building and a third needs it to feel appreciated. However, regardless of the reason, workers require motivation at work and good leaders provide that motivation so those workers can see the value of themselves and their accomplishments.

Soft skilled leaders are in tune with the needs of their employees and they know how to motivate those employees to work toward achieving organizational goals and objectives. They use praise as a tool for getting people to buy into basic management philosophies, they offer support by asking employees what they need to properly perform their jobs, and they provide feedback so employees know where they need to improve.

Without a doubt, soft skilled leaders are the best leaders for motivating employees. Their personalities are naturally geared toward treating people with respect and showing compassion for them as they work through the everyday challenges of their jobs. In short, they know how to inspire people because they understand their personal and professional needs.

Trust builders

As many people are aware, trust building is a challenging endeavor. It takes time and effort to create the relationships necessary to establish trust, and that trust can be broken with a single action.

Communication is the biggest factor involved in building trust, and it starts with leadership. Employees lose trust when leaders do not communicate with them. They want truthful information about their organizations so they know what is happening within them. Without leadership communication, employees are lost without a guide.

Trust also leads to the establishment of culture. Every organization has unique experiences, philosophies, behaviors, norms, and values. They also have specific methods and patterns for interacting with suppliers, customers, employees, and the community. When combined, these attributes define an organization and make up its culture.

Culture starts at the top of an organization and works its way down to lower-level employees. Employees help establish behaviors and norms, but they do not have the same power as those in the upper levels of the established hierarchy. Top ranking members are the only people who have the authority, influence, and control needed to create the overall culture of the organization.

Leaders need employees to trust them or they will not achieve the goals that they have set for their organizations. In fact, trust is one of the most important aspects of leadership because it is difficult, if not impossible, to repair once it is broken.

Employees trust leaders with soft skills because those leaders are empathetic and think before they react. They think about how they would feel if something was done to them that they are about to do to others. For example, before telling employees they are doing a bad job, they think of things that they are also doing well in order to mitigate the harshness of the reprimands.

Soft skilled leaders also understand the importance of maintaining trust once it has been established. They know that employees who lose faith in their actions will also lose faith in their organizations. If this happens, then those organizations risk failure and might cease to exist.

Soft skilled leaders have an advantage over other leaders when it comes to trust. They behave in ways that draw their employees toward them and help those employees believe in the goals and objectives that they have established. Hard skills are great for many aspects of management in organizations, but they cannot compare to the positive effects of soft skills.

Team players

Teams are the major building blocks of many different types of organizations. They have replaced individuals in an attempt to satisfy complex customer demands and resolve internal issues. They utilize personnel who help solve problems faster and more accurately. These personnel are selected based on their position, skill, knowledge, and capacity to lead others. The assembled team is well equipped to find solutions to problems based on their experience, understanding, and capability.

The advantages of teams make it important for leaders to work in, with, and around them. Some of the major advantages are discussed below.

Synergy

This might be the biggest advantage of teams because every member can exchange thoughts and entertain others' perspectives. Each employee has unique strengths that add diversity to the team, and the differing viewpoints contribute to the overall effectiveness. The synergy involved improves decision-making and helps the team reach goals within limited time frames. Soft skilled leaders add to this synergy by motivating team members to express their thoughts and ideas.

Efficiency

Teams are able to move faster and more effectively than individuals acting alone. This is because they make the most of member's individual strengths and talents. In areas where some people are weak, others are strong...and their combined efforts work together to solve problems.

The best part about the efficiency of a team is that it gets better as the team bonds. Over time, members learn the strengths of others in the group and utilize those strengths where and when they are needed. Soft skilled leaders use their communication skills to improve bonding between members; thereby increasing the efficiency of the team as a whole.

Flexibility

Different personalities on a team help the team accept change. Some people find change challenging or stressful while others embrace it. This is because people react differently to the same situations based on their perceptions, and those perceptions give teams the flexibility needed to accept change. Since soft skilled leaders do well with change and change implementation, they are a big plus for the flexibility of teams.

Idea generation

People have different experiences that add to the way they think about things. Team members' individual thoughts generate unique ideas that can be bounced off the rest of the group for problem-solving. This process generates the best ideas because they are evaluated by everyone before being implemented as solutions. In terms of idea generation, soft skilled leaders help team members realize the importance of their contributions based on their unique experiences.

Divided responsibilities

Teams divide responsibilities between group members, and this prevents individual employees from being overloaded with work. It also allows members to support each other through cooperation and mutual understanding. In short, dividing responsibilities alleviates the stress associated with being completely responsible for a project. Soft skilled leaders understand the importance of keeping stress levels manageable and they take action to assure those levels do not become excessive.

The above advantages show why "team players" are important in organizations. When teams succeed, all members are rewarded rather than individuals and the end result is increased motivation and job satisfaction for everyone.

Unfortunately, team players can be difficult to find in organizations because employees typically have much more interest in helping themselves than they do in helping others. This might seem rather harsh, but it is true...especially when companies are cutting costs by hiring fewer people and putting pressure on existing employees to do more.

Soft skilled leaders do well managing teams, but they also are excellent team players. They enjoy giving credit to others and know when it is more important to listen rather than act. They allow informal rules to develop within the teams without interjection. These rules guide members on how to share resources and responsibilities, and they provide a roadmap for accomplishing goals and objectives.

One negative aspect of teams is the fact that individuals sometimes lose their creativity. Soft skilled leaders understand the need for creativity and work with members to allow for it. They often sacrifice their own thoughts and ideas to entertain the thoughts and ideas of others so everyone can contribute and feel part of the decision-making process.

Soft skilled leaders also realize that team members require a time period to adjust to each other's work styles and personalities. This period is known as a learning curve, and it is a problem because team members are not productive during it. Valuable resources are tied up during this process, and that can be costly. However, astute team leaders allow it to naturally take place since the end result is worth the time and money spent.

Last, but certainly not least, soft skilled leaders work with team members to prevent a phenomenon known as social loafing. Social loafing occurs when people exert less effort in teams then when working alone and it is a major reason why workplace teams are sometimes less productive than the combined sum of the members working as individuals.

The worst part about social loafers on teams is that they cause resentment and conflict. People doing the majority of work become resentful toward the loafers and the managers who did nothing to control the situation, and this can negatively impact their morale. Soft skilled leaders understand how to draw in social loafers so they become more productive and a viable part of the contribution process.

Emotional intelligence

It would be difficult to write a book about soft skilled leadership without mentioning emotional intelligence because it is a core component of soft skills. Essentially, emotional intelligence is the capacity of someone to understand the feelings of others and control their own feelings. Emotionally intelligent people hear what others are saying and react emphatically without being upset or distraught. This type of behavior is beneficial in organizations because it prevents situations from becoming emotionally charged. Based on this, it is understandable that emotionally intelligent people often rise to leadership roles in organizations.

In terms of leadership, emotional intelligence is the ability to manage feelings and understand the feelings of others. Leaders with high emotional intelligence know what their emotions are capable of doing, and they harness their feelings to prevent negative reactions from others.

Many articles and books have been written about emotional intelligence and many more will be written in the future due to its mainstream popularity. In terms of business, the topic has generated world-wide attention due to its application in all different types of organizations. This book could expand more on emotional intelligence, but it was not written for that purpose. However, a basic understanding of the concept is necessary to see why it is so critical for soft skilled leaders.

Emotional intelligence is a term that was developed by psychologists Peter Salovey and John Mayer...and later popularized by psychologist Daniel Goleman. Essentially, Goleman designated five major components of emotional intelligence. In terms of leadership, these components are:

Self-awareness

This refers to leaders recognizing their own feelings. Leaders who are self-aware are able to identify and monitor their own emotions for control. They are confident, have a good sense of humor, and are aware of how they are perceived by others. Soft skilled leaders are very self-aware of their own emotional responses, and use this to attract employees to themselves and their methods of management.

Self-regulation

This refers to controlling reactions or impulses. Leaders who react quickly often end up saying things that they would not have said if they thought about the situation. Self-regulation makes leaders conscientious about what they are saying, and it prevents them from responding in ways that elevate the negativity of conversations. Soft skilled leaders always think before they react to avoid offending employees or putting them into a situation where they feel powerless.

Motivation

This refers to leaders' self-motivation for self-improvement. It goes above money and status (external rewards) by focusing on things such as satisfaction and happiness (internal rewards). It also includes a strong drive to accomplish goals and objectives regardless of the circumstances. Optimism is critical here...even when leaders are faced with potential failure. Soft skilled leaders know that optimism is critical because employees will follow their lead and behave similarly.

Empathy

This refers to leaders understanding employees' situations and taking a genuine interest in those situations. It often involves "walking a mile in another person's shoes" to fully comprehend their behavior and reactions. This is a very skillful component because it often requires leaders to anticipate other's needs so they can respond appropriately. Empathy is one of the strongest assets of soft skilled leaders and they know how to use it to accomplish the goals of their organizations.

Social skills

This involves leaders picking up on social cues to build relationships and work toward a common goal. It requires active listening and well-thought responding to persuade others and gain their trust. It also involves team-building and collaboration as a method of working with others. Soft skilled leaders have excellent social skills and they use them to build bridges with others.

High emotional intelligence has several other advantages for soft skilled leaders. For example, they are optimistic because they understand employees want optimism in a leader. They also want people in the other management positions to be upbeat because, after all, the feelings of managers eventually trickle down to the rank and file employees.

Another advantage of high emotional intelligence is responsiveness. Soft skilled leaders want feedback from employees, customers, suppliers, and others because they know it is a valuable tool for making changes and improving their organizations. They take that feedback and put it into action. In short, they are responsive in ways that help their organizations.

A third advantage is soft skilled leaders accept responsibility for their mistakes. They are aware that if they try to blame others for their mistakes, then they can cause outrage in their workforces. They understand that they need to own up to the problems they create and they respond appropriately.

The last advantage of high emotional intelligence is Inspiration. Everyone needs motivation at some point in their career, and soft skilled leaders are often the best people to provide that motivation. They are at the top of the company, and their comments are taken very seriously by all employees. A pat on the back goes a long way...especially when it comes from the leadership of the organization.

A lot more could be said about the importance of emotional intelligence, but the point here is to show how it is innate for soft skilled leaders. The importance of this concept is best summed up by modifying the old American Express phrase, "emotional intelligence, don't leave home without it."

Understanding social responsibility

Social responsibility is an obligation to behave in ways that positively impact society. For leaders of organizations, this means that profit is not their only concern. In fact, in some cases, profitability can take a backseat to assuring nothing harmful is done to society.

Some business leaders find it difficult to put any aspect of business on the same level as financial success. After all, money drives organizations because, without it, those organizations would cease to exist. However, it has been suggested that social responsibility leads to profitability because many socially responsible thoughts and ideas are generated by the public...and companies that ignore those thoughts and ideas have difficulty selling their products and services.

Businesses become socially responsible in one of two ways. The first way involves internal actions that make sure the organization or the people in it do not engage in any type of socially harmful actions. An example is a foundry that invites the EPA to inspect the soil on their property for contamination that might harm the environment. This inspection is not required, but it goes "above and beyond" to protect the environment. The second way involves external actions that do something to directly advance socially responsible goals and objectives. An example is an oil company that invests money, time, and effort into wildlife preservation activities. They did not do any damage to the wildlife that they are working toward preserving, but they want to show that they are concerned about the environment and take appropriate action to highlight that concern.

Social responsibility for businesses came into the spotlight a few decades ago and it has continued to attract attention and grow in popularity. In the early 1990s, Archie Carroll developed a socially responsible pyramid that defined four basic corporate responsibilities. This pyramid has basic stakeholder responsibilities at the bottom (legal and economic) and higher societal responsibilities (ethical and philanthropic) at the top. Similar to

Abraham Maslow's Hierarchy of Needs, lower-level responsibilities of organizations must be met before moving on to the responsibilities that benefit society.

For this book, the social responsibilities of Carroll's pyramid are listed separately without regard to the importance of progression. An additional responsibility that addresses volunteering has also been added for better understanding. That being said, social responsibilities are as follows:

Economic

This is probably the most well-known type of social responsibility, and it refers to an organization's responsibilities to its stakeholders. Businesses are obligated to create jobs, offer valuable products and services, and provide a return-on-investment to stockholders and investors. Organizations must also operate as effectively and efficiently as possible while offering innovative products and services. Most business leaders understand this type of social responsibility and make it one of their top priorities because it helps grow their organizations and sustain their livelihoods.

An example of economic social responsibility is a grocery store chain that enters the high-end market of organic foods. They know organic items are very trendy and profitable, and selling them will positively impact their bottom line. This keeps the company healthy and makes shareholders happy.

Ethical

This type of social responsibility is growing in importance. Organizations are held accountable for the ways they treat the environment, employees, suppliers, customers, and the general public. They are expected to recycle, properly dispose of waste, be fair to their employees, and be truthful to customers about products or services. They are also expected not to play favorites due to friendships, family relationships, or romances. In short, this responsibility involves refraining from behavior that is questionable even though it is not necessarily illegal and acting responsibly in all situations. Sometimes this means going above and beyond what is required by the law.

An example of ethical social responsibility is an accounting firm that offers paid maternity leave to men and women. This is not required by law, but it is an ethical action that allows parents to spend time with new babies without worrying about finances. This shows that the company respects its employees and is concerned about their happiness and well-being.

Legal

Legal social responsibilities cannot be ignored because they are required by law. Organizations need to obey all laws established by the government. Government agencies that enforce laws include the Internal Revenue Service (IRS), Occupational Safety and Health Administration (OSHA), National Labor Relations Board (NLRB), and the Securities and Exchange Commission (SEC).

An example of legal social responsibility is a pawn shop that keeps accurate track of all cash sales as required by law. Cash transactions can be difficult for the IRS to verify, so the pawnshop makes sure these sales are transparent to avoid scrutiny or an audit. They make sure they adhere to the law by doing the right thing.

Philanthropic

This type of social responsibility involves promoting causes that organizations believe are justifiable. It is typically done by giving money in the form of donations, but it can also be in the form of services. Either way, the giving reflects well on the perception of organizations because they are viewed as being charitable.

An example of philanthropic social responsibility is an automotive supplier matching 100 percent of employee monetary donations to the St. Jude Children's Hospital. This action shows compassion and is for a good cause. It also encourages employees to donate by making them feel that their donations are important.

Volunteer

Volunteer social responsibilities do not involve the direct giving of money. Instead, employees offer their services for something that their employer believes is justifiable. This reflects well on the perception of organizations, and it gets people personally involved in a good cause.

An example of volunteer social responsibility is a pharmaceutical company that recruits its employees to work at local soup kitchens. This action shows compassion for those who are less fortunate and it benefits the community. It also benefits the employees because they feel like they are doing something good for the community.

Social responsibility requires a big monetary commitment from organizations, and that commitment presents challenges...especially when profits are low. However, the impact on organizations is far more than financial. It affects employees, customers, suppliers, and the public in positive and negative ways depending on perception as shown below.

Customers

This refers to the retention of current customers and the acquisitions of new ones. Some people simply will not buy products or services from organizations that they do not believe are socially responsible. Instead, they patronize businesses that share similar values.

This type of impact can have a "trickle-down" effect that goes quite deep. For example, a person might refuse to eat at a restaurant because the chicken that the restaurant sells comes from a farm that raises birds in cages rather than letting them live "free-range" style. This action directly impacts the restaurant, but it also indirectly affects the distributor that delivers the chicken, the processor that prepares the chicken, the slaughterhouse that kills the chicken, and the farmer that raises the chicken. In this case, the impact of the person's action is much deeper than it might appear on the surface.

Investment

Investors are needed by many companies, and social responsibility affects those investors. This effect can be positive or negative, depending on perception. For example, an investor might be looking for a company to put money into that is concerned about the environment. They will not invest in a business that is socially irresponsible in terms of the ecosystem....regardless of the potential for return-on-investment.

Like it or not, entire communities are sometimes affected by investment decisions. Small towns rely on businesses to support their economies because those businesses create jobs and generate tax revenue. If a company falls short of receiving an investment due to its inability to be socially responsible, then it can damage the financial well-being of many people who have nothing in common with that company other than to live in the same community.

Image

Every marketing professor knows the importance of image. In their minds, image makes or breaks organizations. Undoubtedly, social responsibility affects the image of companies all over the world. For example, "sweatshops" in other nations that employ people at very low wages are frowned upon by people who are concerned about human rights and violations of ethical social responsibility. Along the same lines, an embezzlement scandal makes a financial institution look bad due to a disregard for economic social responsibility. In short, social responsibility forms images of organizations in people's minds...and a negative image can be very difficult to change.

An example of a negative image is a pharmaceutical company that keeps prices high on drugs that people need to survive so shareholders can profit immensely. This company has little concern for the individuals who need their medication, and the public perceives it as having an image of being uncaring and greedy. This image will be hard to change even if the company takes steps to replace economic social responsibility with ethical social responsibility.

Recruitment

As noted above, social responsibility is directly related to image. That image is ingrained in people's minds, and it is hard to alter. That image also drives the recruitment process because organizations with positive images are attractive to some potential employees. For example, younger employees often place high importance on the ecosystem. They prefer to work for organizations that are environmentally socially responsible, and they will not consider employment with companies that have little regard for the environment.

Recruitment is influenced by the social responsibility of organizations more than many people realize. This is because some people's thinking is subliminal based on the values they have had in place since childhood. They instinctively react to situations based on their values, and this will not change unless their self-awareness is modified by some type of external stimuli or source.

Goals

Social responsibility is important for the establishment of goals and objectives. For example, if leaders of an organization have a goal of making a difference in society, they can achieve it using philanthropic social responsibility. They simply pick a charitable organization and give money to it while encouraging their employees to donate. In this regard, social responsibility encourages organizations to get better and look better in the eyes of outsiders.

Conflict

As some people have likely experienced, social responsibility can create warring factions in organizations. This is due to the fact that the people involved with the specific types of social responsibility are not of the same mindset. For example, economic social responsibility puts profitability above everything else; which does not work well for those concerned with ethical or philanthropic social responsibility. This creates conflict and, unfortunately, that conflict can become dysfunctional. Dysfunctional conflict is destructive because position becomes more important than principle...and then people are attacked instead of the problem. These personal attacks are always negative, and nothing constructive gets accomplished. In short, the tension resulting from different types of social responsibility leads to dysfunctional conflict and long-lasting problems that are difficult to resolve.

Leadership and social responsibility

Leaders all over the world are beginning to realize the importance of making their organizations socially responsible. They know that the choices they make in terms of social responsibility will directly impact the choices their customers make about purchasing their products and services.

Astute leaders understand the potentially negative impact of social responsibility if they choose to ignore it, but this is not the only reason they have for embracing it. Social responsibility provides several other benefits for organizations. This should not come as a surprise, but most people do not realize these benefits because they associate social responsibility with increased costs. Sometimes this is true, but certain companies become more profitable by being socially responsible because the changes they undergo project a more positive image to stakeholders and the public.

In terms of leadership, the major advantages of social responsibility are as follows:

Reputation

There is an old saying that reputation follows people wherever they go. This saying is also true for organizations...but it needs to be expanded upon because, after a while, reputation progresses from a following to a leading role. It leads some companies to growth and prosperity, while it leads others to their graves.

Social responsibility establishes reputations because people see and hear things that influence their thinking. If they see a company donate to charity on a regular basis, then they think highly of that organization. On the other hand, if they see a company where greed drives executives at the expense of others, then they think negatively about that organization.

In short, reputation is an important part of perception that is driven by social responsibility. Leaders that realize this importance find their organizations' socially responsible actions advantageous because they are viewed in a positive light by others.

Customer relationships

Socially responsible leaders build good relationships internally and externally. They establish a rapport with the charities they support, understand the needs of their stakeholders, and work well with the government agencies that regulate their actions. These relationships help build trust with customers because those customers understand the organizations they purchase suppliers and services from are legally, ethically, and economically responsible. Trust leads to the loyalty necessary for repeat business, and it prevents customers from looking for new companies to buy from just because they are less expensive. In short, social responsibility is advantageous because it helps establish and maintain solid customer relationships.

Compliance

Legal social responsibility is great for keeping organizations in compliance with rules and regulations. This is critical because violations cost money, and they can completely stop companies from operating. When companies are compliant, their efficiency also improves so leaders can focus on doing their jobs rather than dealing with enforcement officers or auditors.

Compliance also reduces worry because there is no concern that regulatory actions could be around the corner. This is a significant benefit because worry leads to stress...and stress causes employees to burn out. In the long run, morale is increased, turnover is reduced, and the knowledge employees have acquired remains with their organizations.

Innovation

Innovation is necessary for the growth and prosperity of organizations. This innovation does not necessarily have to be cutting edge, but it needs to be present in some form. Innovation takes companies to the next level using new concepts and ideas, and it tends to snowball once it begins.

Astute leaders realize that social responsibility helps people in their organizations become more innovative. It does this by forcing people to move outside of their comfort zones and still meet goals....often in ways that were never previously considered. For example, in the 1970s, the government forced automobile manufacturers to meet new fuel economy standards. Engineers started working on reducing the weight of cars so they would require less gas to operate. This led to the development of stronger, lighter, and more flexible materials that helped meet the new standards. However, an added plus was that these materials were also cheaper, which lead to a cost-saving that was previously unrealized.

Planning

At first glance, this might not appear to be an advantage. After all, leadership planning in organizations should occur regardless of whether or not socially responsible actions are taking place. However, social responsibility promotes long-term planning because it forces leaders to think about the future so they can maintain their current status. They need to think strategically about ways to incorporate socially responsible actions into the long-term growth of their organizations. This prevents them from focusing only on the short-term goals, such as profitability and return-on-investment, that are most important to investors and stockholders...and it benefits their organizations as a whole because a variety of different factors are taken into consideration.

One problem associated with social responsibility is that cost can get out of hand if it is not monitored closely by leaders. Programs designed to reduce environmental destruction though ethical practices or prevent disease through philanthropic actions can be expensive with no real way to recoup the money spent. This can cause companies a variety of different problem including the inability to meet financial obligations.

This type of problem can have a huge impact on small companies with limited financial resources. They need money in more important areas of their businesses so they can continue to operate, even though their customers and the public might believe otherwise.

Another problem expands on the cost issue, and it might be the most common negative associated with social responsibility. Leaders of organizations have a fiduciary obligation to watch out for the best interests of stockholders, and that obligation is sometimes tossed aside in favor of social responsibility. Stockholders usually buy stock in a company because they want to earn income on the money they have invested. They want a return-on-investment (ROI), and that ROI is hindered by social responsibility because it does not produce income...at least in the short-term. In fact, some types of social responsibility, such as charitable donations, never generate income that can be readily seen. There are tax deductions for these types of financial transactions, but their impact on the bottom line is typically not good.

Not surprisingly, stockholders are often the most vocal opponents of social responsibility. They do not like seeing money come out of their pockets and put into something that might or might not be beneficial. Unfortunately, this issue will likely never go away as long as organizations continue to spend money on socially responsible actions.

The last problem associated with social responsibility is known as groupthink. Psychologist Irving Janis established the term "Groupthink" to describe a process in which a group can make irrational decisions. In these situations, group members attempt to conform to what they believe to be the consensus of the group. The end result is the group ultimately agreeing on something that each member might normally view as unwise. This defeats the entire purpose of team decision making in organizations because ideas are stymied and synergy is virtually non-existent.

Groupthink causes two different and opposite problems. The first problem involves companies becoming too engrossed in social responsibility. For example, the CEO of a bank holds a meeting with all vice presidents to discuss social responsibility of the organization. The CEO strongly believes the bank needs to give more money to charities, and she suggests giving $1,000,000 to breast cancer research. This seems excessive to many the vice presidents...especially since the bank already gives over $300,000 annually to other charities. However, none of the vice presidents speak up or disagree. In fact, they all state that this is a good idea because they do not want to offend the CEO or the other vice presidents. They unanimously agree to donate the breast cancer research money, and the meeting adjourns.

In reality, the bank is very socially responsible because they already give generously to charity. The vice presidents agreed to the $1,000,000 breast cancer research donation even though many of them thought it was unnecessary and excessive. They conformed to what they believed was the consensus of the CEO and the other vice presidents, thereby destroying the benefits of group synergy. In this situation, the bank is too engrossed in social responsibility and they could jeopardize their financial well-being with their actions.

The second problem occurs when groupthink causes companies to not do enough in terms of social responsibility. For example, managers of a restaurant chain meet at the headquarters to evaluate the social responsibility of the organization. Each manager is afraid to express their personal beliefs because they fear it will offend other managers. Instead, every person in the meeting indicates that the restaurant chain is doing enough in terms of social responsibility because they believe that is what everyone wants to hear. They all agree that nothing else needs to be done, and the meeting adjourns.

In reality, the restaurant chain is doing very little to address social responsibility. The managers agreed that that enough was being done even though some of them thought differently. They conformed to what they believed was the consensus of management, thereby destroying the benefits of synergy that typically come from group decision making. In other words, the meeting did nothing to evaluate the social responsibility of the restaurant chain other than reducing it to an insignificant factor. In this situation, the restaurant chain is not doing enough in terms of social responsibility.

Despite the problems involved, leaders are more and more realizing the importance of social responsibility. They know that they must become more proactive in terms of being socially responsible and this involves innovation and investment. In terms of innovation, they must come up with ways to get better instead of waiting to be told what they need to do. For example, an oil company could contribute to charitable organizations that help wildlife after their habitat has been destroyed. This must be done before, not after, the company has its own oil spill to show that they have invented a way to reach out to the community without being in an emergency situation. This action will reflect well on the oil company if they make a mistake and damage the environment in the future. In short, organizations must be proactive instead of reactive in order to improve their social responsibility.

In terms of investment, leaders need to allocate resources for an ongoing effort to maintain and improve social responsibility. For example, employees can be designated to develop strategies and designate funding for projects that make sure workers find job satisfaction. This falls under ethical social responsibility, and it prevents future problems by addressing issues before they fester into something bigger. In short, a little time and money spent now can prevent a lot of time and money from being spent later on.

Leaders need to spend time, money, and effort in order to move social responsibility forward in their organizations. This might present some challenges in the beginning, but the end results are worth the sacrifice.

The future leader

In the future, leaders will have to be flexible and resourceful in order to meet the challenges they will encounter. Past leaders have faced similar challenges, but the world has changed and so have leadership responsibilities. Quite simply, employees are more complex, rules are more stringent, and more productivity must be achieved with fewer resources.

Please consider the following in regard to the changes that leaders face now and will take into the future:

Employees

- Employees do not remain at one place of employment as long as they did in the past. For example, the elimination of most pension plans took away a big incentive for people to continue working for the same company.
- Workers want more family time than they did in the past. For example, paternity leave (father's leave for a new child) was virtually unheard of in the past, but it has become somewhat common today.
- Women and minorities are advancing in management positions. For example, it is no longer uncommon to find a female CEO in a large company.

Rules

- Environmental laws are becoming more stringent. For example, the push toward "green" is forcing companies to take measures to clean up their pollutants.
- Discrimination issues are becoming more prevalent. For example, age discrimination lawsuits are becoming more common as older employees are forced out for lower-paid younger workers.
- Safety precautions are becoming more mandatory. For example, safety requirements facing the automotive industry are continually increasing to protect the people who drive their vehicles.

Productivity

- Lean management is becoming the norm. For example, it is now expected for workers to take on additional job responsibilities without increased compensation.
- Just in time inventory is becoming mandatory. For example, companies today are continually calculating the cost of inventory and holding employees accountable for high numbers.
- Automation is becoming part of the status quo. For example, unions are now giving in to the incorporation of machinery used to replace humans in the workforce.

All of the above changes factor into the profitability of organizations. However, future leaders of organizations will realize that profitability must also take into account the triple-bottom-line, a term first described by John Elkington in the mid-1990s, in order to get a more accurate picture of organizational success or failure.

The triple bottom line factors in the environment and society that, along with income and sales, make up the value of businesses and determine profitability. It was developed by social scientists and is used by those who believe profitability is defined by a broader concept that takes society and the environment into account. It considers the direct and indirect costs of financial, environmental, and social impacts to be the three major factors for determining profitability.

An example of a business adhering to the triple-bottom-line concept is a company that invests fifty percent of all profits back into the local community. This company employs refugees from war-torn nations who are assigned the responsibility of collecting metal scrap and recycling it for cash. Society benefits from the employment found for disadvantaged refugees, the local community benefits from the donations received, the environment benefits from the recycling, and the business benefits from the profits they keep. Essentially, everyone wins in what should be a long-term endeavor.

One major challenge associated with the triple-bottom-line is that it can be difficult to accurately measure the value of the social and environmental impact. Green business is based on minimizing the negative impact, and this is difficult to gauge because the maximum impact of those negatives is unknown. This means some guesswork must be involved, and guesswork is frowned upon by number-crunching people who prefer quantitative results supported by real data.

Leaders will also need to consider sustainability in addition to the social responsibility of their organizations. Sustainability is the thinking that everything people need is based on the natural environment, and they must find harmony with that environment in order to survive and thrive. One hand washes the other as humans and nature work to benefit each other. For example, people need to breathe air so they must make sure that air is kept clean for use. If that air is too polluted, then the future of humanity is at risk.

Many of the policies related to sustainability were established by environmentalists, but over time this thinking has become part of the mainstream. The United States made sustainability a national policy in 1969 by enacting the National Environmental Policy Act. This law allows the government to oversee the environmental, social, and economic impact of human actions by implementing regulations, funding private projects, constructing public facilities, and managing the usage of land.

The branch of government responsible for establishing and enforcing rules and regulations related to sustainability is the Environmental Protection Agency (EPA).   The EPA upholds this responsibility based on the following principles:

- Protect and replenish natural resources related to water, land, air, and energy.
- Fund and support positive outcomes for environmental, social, and economic systems.
- Prevent and reduce waste, pollution, and contamination related to natural resources and the environment.

Other nations have followed the general practices of sustainability for hundreds of years, even though most of them do not have writing policies that document their commitment. These nations' actions speak louder than their words, and some of those actions came about out of sheer necessity. For example, Europeans adhered to rules of environmental conservation because they knew that they could not exist without the resources that the earth provided. Those resources were renewable, but only if a plan was in place to make sure a conservation protocol was followed. Sustainability allowed people to live off the land and it assured that future generations could do the same.

In business, sustainability is similar to social responsibility because both are concerned with society and organizations benefiting from the programs that are in place. However, there is a difference between these two terms because social responsibility focuses on the present, where sustainability is more about the future. For example, a lumber yard might feel a social responsibility to purchase all wood from nations with concern for human rights. However, from a sustainability standpoint, that same lumber yard might want to prevent the world's rain forests from being over-harvesting in order to protect them from becoming extinct. In short, social responsibility is geared toward short-term results while sustainability is concerned with long-term outcomes.

Like it or not, organizational leaders are going to have to think about the long term effects of their decisions. Social responsibility will not be enough to satisfy people as they learn more about the impact that organizational actions have on the environment. Sustainability will grow in importance and leaders will have to make changes to meet the demands that come along with that growth.

Another concern that future organizational leaders will have to address involves the ethical actions, or more importantly unethical actions, of their organizations. Future leaders will need to handle these types of situations delicately to avoid having them blow up into even bigger issues, and those with the best soft skills and highest emotional intelligence have the ability to do so.

Organizational ethics are formal and informal guidelines designed to regulate employee actions. They describe how people should behave in the workplace and combat employee activities that management deems unacceptable. In short, these guidelines establish ideas of right and wrong and need to be followed because unethical actions set undesirable precedents.

Undesirable precedents can develop in a relatively short period of time, and they can cause multiple problems if they are allowed to continue. Employees who witness unethical behavior might assume it is acceptable and start doing it themselves. The end result can be a downward spiral for the organization and the people working in it. For example, a clerical worker chooses to read novels for personal enjoyment instead of doing her job when the office manager is not in the office. Other clerks see her behavior and also begin to do personal tasks when the boss is away. This prevents necessary office work from being completed in a timely manner and slowly starts negatively affecting other departments in the company.

Leaders of the future will realize that workplace ethics are significant because they affect the health and profitability of organizations. They determine proper ways for employees to conduct themselves in specific situations and define ideas of excellence, justice, virtue, right, and wrong. They are important to the organization and the community it resides in.

Unethical behavior is not always crystal clear. Some things that appear to be unethical might actually not be...especially when culture comes into play. Bribery, for example, might be considered unethical in the United States, but it is a conventional practice in other nations. In fact, bribes are regularly accepted and largely go unnoticed.

Sometimes, they are even expected in order to conduct business, and people are offended if this protocol is not followed. This indicates that there might be times in business when the situation needs to be considered before personal beliefs and/or values.

Historically, there have been many different types of unethical behavior in organizations. Corporations have dumped millions of gallons of waste into oceans and waterways, spewed pollution into the air, and left tons of waste in landfills where it does not decompose. Other companies have overcharged the government for health-related procedures, overbilled insurance companies, and used tax-deductible donations for personal gain of employees.

Unfortunately, these types of unethical and unlawful business methods exist, but why is this so? What are the reasons for the wrong actions committed by these organizations? The answer, not surprisingly, involves money. It's much less expensive to dump waste in an ocean than it is to have it picked up and properly disposed of, and billing the government for services that were never performed is virtually 100 percent profit. Bribes and payoffs are also easy money that can be generated for long periods of time. As long as both parties involved willingly consent, this unethical activity can go on indefinitely.

Unfortunately, unethical organizations provide a lifestyle that reinforces illicit activities. They even recruit employees who have the same mindset for dishonest behavior, and those employees immediately become an active part of the culture.

Whistleblowers, or people who tell authorities about corporate wrongdoing, are able to stop some unethical issues with their reporting. These individuals can be customers, suppliers, employees, or someone on the streets who witnesses unethical activities. Their work is admirable and justified, but it also involves risk. They stick their necks out, and they can be punished or ostracized by those who are profiting from the wrongful activities. It might seem hard to believe, but whistleblowers are often chastised for doing the right thing...and that prevents many from taking the appropriate action.

Unethical actions in the workplace can affect employees and the organizations where they work. Future leaders will realize that are many problems that can result from ethical violations. One problem involves legal issues including lawsuits, fines, and imprisonment. Organizations that are part of unethical activities might be sued by the affected parties if those parties find that activity detrimental. Nobody wants to be on the receiving end of a lawsuit. Even if they win, they still have to spend money and time proving their innocence. Fines from regulating bodies might also be imposed due to legal issues. If the government determines an organization has violated established rules and regulations pertaining to ethics, there is little they can do to combat the fines levied against them due to the cost involved. Last, and often times most important, employees can go to prison for unethical activity.

Public relations issues are an additional problem that can result from ethical violations. The internet and social media spread news very quickly...regardless of whether that news is good or bad. When unethical activities of organizations go public, the perception of that organization becomes negative. This can be a very challenging situation to get out of and that is why big companies spend so much money on public relations campaigns that prevent this type of trouble.

Another issue that can result from ethical fiascos involves productivity. Employees who witness unethical behavior in organizations are less committed to those organizations. The dishonest activities they observe lower their morale and reduce their respect for the leaders that should be taking control of the problem. Ultimately, they lose motivation, and this lack of motivation results in reduced output

Last, but certainly not least, future leaders of organizations will have to pay much closer attention to their employees' mental and physical health. This includes things such as stress, information overload, high blood pressure, and heart attacks that result from excessive workload and exhaustion. Once again, leaders with soft skills and high emotional intelligence will perform best with these types of issues because they have empathy for people and listen to what they truly need to improve their jobs and reduce the potential for health-related problems.

When problems arise that result in serious health concerns, soft skilled leaders are the best choice for diffusing the situations. For example, an active shooter has the potential to harm or kill many people in an organization. If that shooter feels that he is being heard and understood by the leader of that organization, there is a chance that he might discontinue his attack. This is never guaranteed, but a hard-core approach has a much lower chance of being successful.

A section on leaders of the future would not be complete without discussing leadership style. A crystal ball is needed to know exactly what these leaders will be like and how they will manage, but it can be said with confidence that they will move away from authoritarian and transactional styles of leadership. They will not keep a tight leash on employees and strict policies and procedures will be limited to the areas where they are most needed such as safety, discrimination, and dishonesty. They will also shy away from standardized practices and systems that hold people accountable for achieving goals and objectives. Instead, the soft skills and emotional intelligence of these leaders will result in their styles being more transformational and democratic. They will work tirelessly to get people to think independently and transform them into workers who want to improve themselves and their organizations. While this transformation is taking place, employees will be encouraged to share decision-making responsibilities with their coworkers and avoid strict protocols that allow only a select few to have decision-making authority.

Summary

This book examines the influence soft skills and social responsibility on leaders of the future. It is an excellent reference for beginners or those seeking general knowledge because the material is written for easy comprehension. It also provides real-world examples for clarity and understanding; thereby providing a simple explanation of subject matter that can be rather complex.

The book is divided into six parts including (1) understanding soft skills, (2) leadership and soft skills, (3) emotional intelligence, (4) understanding social responsibility, (5) leadership and social responsibility, and (6) the future leader. Each section provides valuable information about the designated topic and information flows logically from one part to the next; thereby providing a smooth transition of all written material.